CU00405169

# fantastic ideas for
# exploring nature

KATE BASS AND JANE VELLA

Featherstone
An imprint of Bloomsbury Publishing Plc

50 Bedford Square          1385 Broadway
London                     New York
WC1B 3DP                   NY 10018
UK                         USA

www.bloomsbury.com

First published 2015

British Library Cataloguing-in-Publication Data
A catalogue record for this book is available from the British Library.

ISBN:
PB 978-1-4729-1920-5
ePDF 978-1-4729-1921-2

Library of Congress Cataloging-in-Publication Data
A catalogue record for this book is available from the Library of Congress.

10 9 8 7 6 5 4 3 2 1

Printed and bound in India by Replika Press Pvt Ltd.

This book is produced using paper that is made from wood grown in managed, sustainable
forests. It is natural, renewable and recyclable. The logging and manufacturing processes
conform to the environmental regulations of the country of origin.

To view more of our titles please visit www.bloomsbury.com

**Acknowledgements**
With special thanks to Summerside Primary School and Whipperley Infant Academy and their
families who supported us with such fabulous photographs.

# Contents

# Introduction

In these days of diminishing budgets, our early years team set out to substitute costly and limited plastic teaching equipment for natural recycled and homemade resources. Though initially born out of necessity, we also recognised that these resources are much more than an economy; they are robust, attractive, natural, lovely to hold and manipulate and a tremendous opportunity for learning.

Of course, using natural resources has long been part of the Montessori and Steiner philosophies and some mainstream early years provisions are already emulating this practice.

In this modern world, with the rise of childhood obesity, it is never too early to instil a love and appreciation of the beauty of nature. With the arrival of the internet, digital TV and computer games, our children are becoming less active and sadly less imaginative.

As Albert Einstein said:

> 'Imagination is more important than knowledge. For knowledge is limited to all we now know and understand, while imagination embraces the entire world and all there ever will be to know and understand.'

When children are bored there are a wealth of high cost gadgets to entertain them but it is a privilege to be able to give children opportunities to explore the simpler things in life. We ourselves remember with fondness the thrill of climbing trees, damming streams, playing Robin Hood and caring for a pet stone! In this book we have tried to capture our philosophy of giving children the opportunities that a natural based education can bring.

The activities included here allow children to explore the processes and experiences of the natural world around them. Practitioners are able to spend time developing the children's problem solving and thinking skills, rather than focusing on the end product. These open-ended resources allow children opportunities to take their learning forward in a variety of meaningful contexts. Although focused on the natural world, many of these activities can take place both in and outside. Practitioners can use these activities to assess children across all seven areas of the Early Years Foundation Stage as well as the Characteristics of Effective Learning.

## The structure

The activities all follow the same format:

- 'What you need' lists the items required for the activity, and these are all readily available at home.

- 'What to do' gives step-by-step instructions for completing the task.

- 'Taking it forward' contains some more ideas for additional activities on the same theme. They have been designed to extend and broaden the children's experiences.

- 'What's in it for the child?' is a brief statement that indicates how the activities contribute to learning.

- 'Top tip' offers a brief suggestion, warning or piece of advice to help in tackling the activity.

- A 'Health & Safety' warning (where appropriate) lists any specific hazards involved in completing that activity.

## Food allergy alert

When using food produce to enhance your play opportunities, always be mindful of potential food allergies. Look out for this symbol on the relevant pages.

## Skin allergy alert

Some detergents and soaps can cause skin reactions. Always be aware of potential skin allergies when letting children mix materials with their hands, and always provide facilities for children to wash their hands afterwards. Watch out for this symbol on the relevant pages.

## Safety issues

Children may need to be reminded to wash their hands when using natural materials or preparing food. They may also need reminding not to put things in their mouths, and to be told to be extra careful with real-life or found resources.

SAFETY FiRST!

# Bark rubbing

- Suitable trees!
- Wax crayons
- Paper, not too thick
- String

## Taking it forward

- Encourage the children to label their rubbings with the type of tree.

- Compare rubbings from different trees. Which bark patterns make the nicest rubbings? Can you tell which rubbings came from which kind of tree? Can you make it into a game?

- Try taking a leaf rubbing from a variety of trees.

- Use the rubbings to make a non-fiction group book about trees. Include some interesting facts about the trees.

## What to do:

1. Talk to the children about the bark of the trees and notice the different types of bark, from a relatively smooth beech to a knobbly old oak.

2. Choose a tree.

3. Place the paper on the tree trunk and tie it to the tree with the string.

4. Rub the crayon across it using the flattened side, keeping the strokes in one direction, until the pattern of the bark can be clearly seen.

## What's in it for the children?

This activity introduces children to a variety of patterns and textures in our environment. This will help them to understand how plants have different features to enable them to live in a range of environments. This could easily be used as a creative activity by introducing different colours to use for their rubbings.

## Top tip ⭐

Don't try to do this in the rain!

# Clay impressions

## What you need:

- Bag or container each
- Selection of natural objects, such as leaves, ferns, flowers, pine cones and acorns
- Clay

## Top tip ⭐

Teach the children to store any unused clay by rolling it into small balls and making a well with their thumbs. Top the well up with water and keep in a sealed bucket, ready for next time.

### Taking it forward

- Make two impressions of each object to play a matching game.
- Use a straw to push a small hole in each disc before it hardens, so they can be threaded onto string to hang.

### What's in it for the children?

Clay, like sand and water, has a natural appeal and can easily be shaped and moulded. Children can roll, flatten, poke and squeeze the clay, which is a great way to improve both fine and gross motor skills. By taking an imprint the children will be able to look closely at the features of each object and talk about how one may vary from another.

### ➕ Health & Safety

Always ensure children are careful about picking up unknown objects and wash their hands when they return indoors. Advise them not to put their fingers in their mouths when they have been handling natural items outdoors.

## What to do:

1. Give the children a bag or container and ask them to collect interesting leaves, ferns, flowers, pine cones and acorns etc. Then talk about what they have found.
2. Get the children to each mould a small piece of clay into a ball.
3. Place the natural object on a flat surface and put the ball of clay on top.
4. Press down on the ball, then lift up to reveal the imprint left in the clay.
5. Allow the clay to dry and allow the children to paint or varnish if they wish.

# Nature's paintbrushes

## What you need:

- Sticks
- Plant cuttings
- Scissors
- Elastic bands

## What to do:

1. Ask the children to collect some sticks, not too thin or wide and as straight as possible.

2. Allow the children to snip off some bushy plant cuttings. They won't need a lot.

3. Get them to trim their cuttings so they are the same length and then bunch them together.

4. They may need some help to attach the bunch to the end of the stick by wrapping the elastic band around it several times.

5. Demonstarte how they have made a kind of natural paintbrush!

**Top tip** ⭐

Don't put expectations on the children to create an end product, just allow them to explore the process.

### Taking it forward

- Try using a range of different plant cuttings to explore the different patterns and textures produced.

- Try combining the paintbrushes with the mud paint shown on page 28.

### What's in it for the children?

When working outside, children are less inhibited and more willing to have a go at activities. This is a multi-sensory experience which is open ended. The children will be developing some mathematical understanding and problem solving as they make their own paintbrushes.

# Stick people

## What you need:

- PVA glue
- Paintbrushes or glue spreaders
- A range of sticks
- Fabric scraps
- Googly eyes
- Wool
- Scissors

## What to do:

**1.** Allow the children to explore the resources and give them free rein in designing their own characters.

**2.** Painting the stick with glue will enable them to stick on fabric 'clothes' and wool for hair.

**3.** A small length of wool could be cut and stuck on as a mouth.

**4.** Encourage them to look at each other's faces to help them add features and details to their stick people.

### Top tip ⭐

Try reading **Stick Man** by Julia Donaldson first, to get the children thinking about stick people.

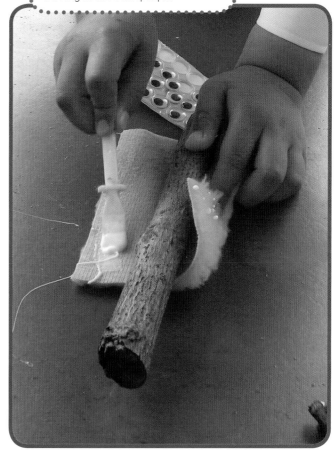

**Taking it forward**

Encourage the children to make a whole family of sticks, thinking about the various sizes they would use to represent different family members.

**What's in it for the children?**

This creative activity offers a fantastic opportunity to discuss difference, exploring families, home and communities. No two sticks are the same, just as no two children are the same!

# Stick rafts

## What you need:

- Some straight sticks
- Long grass stems or twine
- A large leaf for the sail
- A water tray

**Top tip** ⭐

Try using pipe cleaners to join the sticks for younger or less able children.

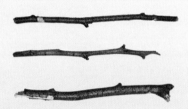

**Taking it forward**

- Try adding small world people or animals to the activity and challenge the children to transport them across the 'river'. How many figures can they fit on their raft before it capsizes? What happens if they put all the figures on one side?

- Get the children to race their rafts – friendly competition has emotional benefits as well.

**What's in it for the children?**

This design and technology activity helps children to explore the concept of buoyancy. What floats? What sinks? Children will be developing their hand-eye coordination as they construct their raft and weave the grasses to join the sticks.

 **Health & Safety**

Always supervise children around water.

## What to do:

1. Choose four sticks of an equal length for the frame. Make a square with the sticks, overlapping the corners.

2. Wind the grass stems or twine around each join, winding from corner to corner in a cross pattern. Do the same for each corner.

3. Once you have made the frame, lay sticks across winding the grass around as you did for the frame.

4. Repeat this until the base is covered.

5. Thread a stick through the large leaf and push between a gap in the sticks to make a sail.

6. The raft is ready for its first voyage in your indoor or outdoor water tray!

# Journey sticks

## What you need:

- Wool or string
- 'Y' shaped sticks
- Natural finds such as leaves, sticks and acorns

## Top tip ⭐

Expose the children to the vocabulary around different emotions before you attempt this activity.

### Taking it forward

- Explain to the children that Native Americans used 'journey sticks' as maps to remind them of routes and tell others about their journey.

- Offer the children lengths of coloured wool and a stick to take with them on your walk. Encourage the children to think about how they are feeling at certain points of their journey and ask them to choose a colour that would best represent how they are feeling.

- When they get back can they articulate how they were feeling during their journey?

### What's in it for the children?

This activity can improve children's memory skills and is an excellent way to keep children interested while walking. It is a fantastic imagination boost and an enhancement for storytelling skills. It is also a great way to introduce maps.

## What to do:

1. Discuss how we find our way – maps, compass, Sat Nav etc. How would we manage without these? Do the children think their memories are good enough to remember a route?

2. Before you set out for your walk together ask the children to wind the wool around the 'Y' end of the stick and tie it on to secure it.

3. As you walk along, encourage the children to look out for interesting finds that they can tuck into their journey stick to remind them of where they have been and what they have seen.

4. At the end of your walk allow the children the opportunity to explain their findings.

# Natural mobiles

## What you need:

- Natural objects such as leaves, feathers, pine cones, sea shells, flower heads etc.
- Large darning needles
- String or wool
- Large stick or branch

## What to do:

1. Gather together some interesting natural objects. Ask the children to look for objects which already have a small hole in them. Can the children work out how to tie the string to them without them falling off?

2. Help the children to thread some lengths of string or wool on to the needles. Let them thread leaves and other objects on to the strings.

3. Get the children working together to attach the threaded or tied objects on to the large stick or branch. They will need to experiment with positioning, to get the stick to balance.

4. Decide together on a good place to hang the mobile.

### Top tip ⭐

If there are any children in your setting who may struggle when using a needle, make this an activity that all can access. Take a pipe cleaner, fold it in half and form a loop at the bend (this is the eye of the needle). Then twist the other ends together to form the needle.

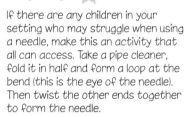

### aking it forward

Make themed or seasonal mobiles by adding photographs or images associated with the found objects. For example a seascape image of children's beach holiday photographs with shells, dried seaweed and driftwood.

Can the children use their phonic knowledge to add key words to thread on?

### 'hat's in it for the children?

obiles are a great way of incorporating ature into any learning environment. hildren will be refining their fine motor kills whilst threading and tying the jects. Problem solving skills will be eveloped as they experiment with the oncept of weight distribution.

# forest faces

## What you need:

- Heavy mud or air-drying clay
- Sandwich bags to store the clay
- Some natural objects you have picked up along your way such as leaves, twigs, pine cones, acorns, feathers, moss, stones etc.
- Camera

### Top tip ⭐

The clay will eventually fall off and integrate with the soil around it. It is important to respect the environment and only use natural materials.

### Taking it forward

- Make mud creatures by moulding the sticky mud to make the body shape. Use natural objects to add features such as legs, wings, teeth, tentacles, eyes, claws etc.

### What's in it for the children?

Clay has very therapeutic qualities. The act of holding clay in your hands can be very calming. Clay has a natural appeal and is quick to mould so children feel like they are in control, and this gives them confidence and an outlet to convey their emotions.

## What to do:

1. Divide the mud or clay into portions and store in sandwich bags to prevent it from drying out.
2. Tell the children to look for natural shapes in the trees that they could incorporate in their designs.
3. Once the children have chosen their tree, give them the mud to push onto the trunk to form the face.
4. They can then use the natural objects to add features.
5. Allow the children to photograph their creations.

# Woodland hunt

## What you need:

- A small bag
- A list of things to find
- A pencil
- Appropriate clothing and footwear

### Taking it forward

- Visit the woods again when the season changes. 'Last time we came to the woods, the trees were full of leaves. Now the branches are bare. Why do you think that is?'

- Point out a piece of litter, ask the children their thoughts. 'Look someone has left a can here. Can you think of some reasons why we should not drop litter?'

### What's in it for the children?

Children need to, and have the desire to, discover the natural world around them. We need to facilitate this by giving them outdoor experiences every day. This is a physical activity that is multi-sensory too, so many areas of development will be explored. What better way to learn about the weather than by experiencing it first hand? The woods can offer a very different learning experience after a shower, in comparison to a visit on a warm, hazy day.

### Health & Safety

Never visit woods on a windy day when falling trees or branches could hurt the children.

## What to do:

1. Write a list of items to find in the woods, include items that require the children to use all their senses, for example: something soft, colourful, spikey, scented, delicate, useful etc.

2. Go for a walk in your local woodland or park with your list and a small bag to collect your found objects.

3. When you arrive in your chosen place, ask the children to close their eyes and say: 'What can you hear? What can you smell?'

4. Look for the items on the list and encourage the children to tick them off as they find them.

5. Discuss other points of interest, for example: look for a felled tree and count the rings to estimate the age of the tree.

6. Provoke discussion by stating 'I think this sapling is about two years old. How old do you think that big oak tree is?'

7. Use vocabulary such as bark, trunk, branch, moss, bird song, nest, hibernate, burrow, mulch, fungi, poisonous, evergreen, camouflage.

# Nature portraits

## What you need:

- A mirror
- Thick paper or card
- PVA glue
- Natural materials such as twigs, leaves, dried grasses, seeds, bark, fir cones, seed cases etc.

## What to do:

1. Ask the children to study themselves in the mirror. What kind of hair do they have? What shape is their face?

2. Leave them to create their self-portraits using the natural resources available.

3. These look great displayed in your setting, mounted on black paper and hanging off large suspended branches with fishing wire.

### Top tip ⭐

This activity can be done on the move as transient art. Just clear an area on the ground to create your self-portrait. Take a photo as a reminder.

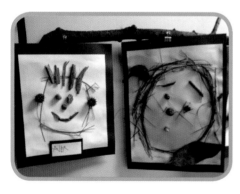

### Taking it forward

- Have children working in pairs to create portraits of each other. Can they say something nice about their friend which you can later add as a quote with their picture?

### What's in it for the children?

Art helps children to test possibilities and work through challenges – they are able to make their own decisions while they learn that a problem may have more than one answer.

# Nest building

## What you need:

- Sticks
- Grass
- Leaves
- Pine needles
- Moss

## What to do:

**1.** Ask the children how they think a bird builds a nest. What could a bird use? Encourage them to think about what they might find in nature that is strong, that is flexible and that a bird can access in the wild.

**2.** Gather the resources together and offer them to the children to have a go at building their own nests.

**3.** Try to get them to think about what kinds of things would help a nest hold its shape.

**4.** Encourage them to weave items together. Can they use just two fingers, like a bird's beak, to get things to stick together?

**5.** When they have finished, ask them to look for some small stones or fir cones that could be the eggs. Can their nest hold them?

**Taking it forward**

Get the children to build their own human-sized nest. They can work in groups. Offer them hay or straw, branches, fallen leaves, shredded paper.

**What's in it for the children?**

This activity allows the children to problem solve using natural objects. It also offers the opportunity to have a discussion about animals in our environment and their natural habitats.

# Making music

## What you need:

- Forked sticks
- Acrylic paint and paintbrushes (optional)
- Brightly coloured buttons
- Jingle bells
- Craft wire
- Coloured wool

## What to do:

**1.** If using paint, offer the children a selection of colours to decorate their stick with. Leave to dry.

**2.** Cut some craft wire for each stick and ask the children to thread on buttons and jingle bells. Looping the wire at one end before threading will prevent the buttons sliding off.

**3.** Help the children to wrap the wire around the forked end of the stick and stretch it across to the other side. Ensure no sharp ends are poking out.

**4.** To make a handle, wrap coloured wool tightly around the stick and tie to secure.

**5.** Your instruments are ready to play!

### Top tip ⭐

Acrylic paints will stain clothes so ensure clothes and surfaces are well covered.

## Taking it forward

■ Make a range of instruments from natural and recycled materials:

- Make a frame of large straight sticks and hang off lengths of the very wide bamboo canes, available at garden centres.

- Make drums with very large catering size cans (ensure edges are not sharp) upturned. Use sticks to hit them with. Challenge children to copy a tapped rhythm. Can they make up their own rhythm?

- Halved coconut shells to tap together are always a hit!

## What's in it for the children?

Music covers all areas of child development and it helps the body and mind work together. This activity promotes creativity, concentration and listening skills.

# Witch's broomstick

## What you need:

- A long straight thick stick
- Lots of smaller, thinner twigs
- String or twine
- Ribbons/streamers

## Top tip ⭐

Soak the sticks in a bucket of water overnight. This will make them easier to bend when making a broom.

## What to do:

1. Ask the children to look for a strong, straight stick to be the broom handle.
2. Collect together a pile of smaller twigs, to make the broom part.
3. Using the string or twine, attach the bundle of twigs securely to one end of the stick to make the broomstick.
4. Decorate with lengths of ribbons or streamers.

### Taking it forward

- This broom is known as a besom broom. The handle is traditionally made from hazel and the head from birch twigs. Use this stimulus to start discussions about witches. Look at stories such as *Room on the Broom* by Julia Donaldson, *Spells* by Emily Gravett, *What's in the Witch's Kitchen?* by Nick Sharratt and the *Winnie the Witch* series by Valerie Thomas and Korky Paul.

### What's in it for the children?

This activity covers both areas of Expressive Arts and Design, initially as the children explore the techniques needed to join the materials and then by using their imaginations to develop role play and stories.

# Shadow faces

## What you need:

- A sunny day!
- A selection of natural objects such as leaves, stones, acorns, fir cones, sticks etc.
- Googly eyes
- A camera

### Top tip ⭐

This may be easier if children work in pairs, taking turns to create shadow pictures or take photographs.

## What to do:

1. Gather together a collection of natural objects to use in your shadow pictures.

2. Tell the children to look for a sunny spot, where their shadow can be easily seen on the ground.

3. Ask them to get into a position where they can reach the shadow of their head without having to change position.

4. Let them use the objects they have collected to add features to their shadow face.

5. Once they are happy with their image they can have it photographed by another person (who must be careful not to cast their own shadow over the picture).

### Taking it forward

■ Experiment with other ways to play with shadows. Try drawing around your own shadow with chalk. Make a sun dial by using an upright length of stick and noting the shadow's position at various times during the day. Talk about the light, light source and whether objects are transparent, translucent or opaque.

### What's in it for the children?

This is a great introduction to the early concept of light and shadows. Adding a camera to capture these transient images offers a perfect opportunity to integrate ICT into the early years curriculum.

# Weaving

## What to do:

1. Ask the children to lay the sticks in place to form a frame. It can be any size or shape – rectangular, square, triangular etc.

2. Help them to join the corners of the frame by wrapping the wool in a criss-cross pattern and tying it off at the back. Repeat until all the sticks are attached. This is their loom.

3. Tie a piece of wool around one of the corners and begin wrapping it around the loom. Wrapping it around the stick twice will keep the wool taught and stop it from sliding on the sticks.

4. Tie the wool off on one of the corners when you reach the other side of the loom.

5. Take the loom on a nature walk. Get the children to collect interesting leaves, grasses, flowers, twigs and seeds etc. that they find on the ground. Weave them through the strings on your loom.

### Top tip ⭐

Try this activity at different times during the year – what the children discover in autumn will be very different from what they find in spring.

### Taking it forward

- Make a really large frame together; willow would be perfect for this. It could be a whole-class project, where the children can weave 'in' and 'out' using their whole bodies.

### What's in it for the children?

Along with offering a sensory, tactile and creative experience, weaving is a fantastic activity to encourage a pincer grip and improve fine motor skills. Weaving also helps hand-eye coordination and aids concentration.

# Leaf threading

## What you need:

- Pom poms
- Googly eyes and short lengths of pipe cleaner
- A selection of different coloured and shaped leaves
- A hole punch
- Sticks, long grass, string or twine

## Top tip ⭐

Try to provide enough hole punches for a small group, as it can be frustrating having to wait for a turn.

## Taking it forward

- Can the children come up with their own criteria for creating a more complicated pattern?

## What's in it for the children?

This activity allows the children time to explore the environment and different leaves, whilst developing muscles in their hands using the hole punch. By using these natural resources children can discuss the mathematical concepts of size, shape and colour. This activity is intentionally open ended, with the emphasis on the process rather than an end product.

## What to do:

1. Glue some pom poms, googly eyes and pipe cleaner antennae onto the top of hand staplers, to make 'hungry caterpillars'.

2. Offer them to the children to punch holes into the leaves ready to thread them. How many holes can they punch in one leaf? Encourage them to experiment with folding soft leaves to see what will happen. Do they notice any symmetry?

3. Allow the children to explore threading the leaves in any way they can come up with. They may wish to thread along the edge of their leaf with a long blade of grass, or thread many leaves onto a stick. Can they make a repeating pattern?

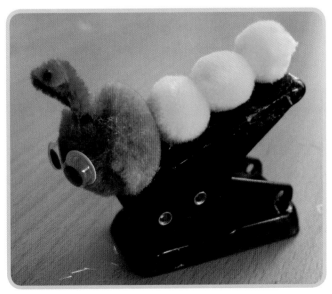

# Flower petal perfume

## What you need:

- Pans
- Flower petals, herbs
- Rotary whisks
- Ladles
- Spoons
- Pestle and mortar
- Pipettes
- Selection of small bottles
- Food colouring
- Sticky labels

## What to do:

1. Offer the children a range of different containers and utensils to create their own perfume.

2. Encourage the children to use a pincer grip to pull off individual petals and add them to water in their pans.

3. Show them how to use the pestle and mortar to crush petals and herbs.

4. Let them add any colour, mix with the whisks or spoons and transfer it with the pipettes to fill their little bottles.

### Top tip ⭐

Try to include a variety of colours and scents to allow for some interesting fragrances.

Taking it forward

- Use the sticky labels to decorate the bottles and give their perfume a name.
- Why not add some glitter to their creation?

What's in it for the children?

By pouring, mixing, sprinkling and squeezing, the children are developing their fine motor skills. The finger-thumb grip needed to use the pipette is similar to the pencil grip, so by using and strengthening these muscles and tendons, the children are developing the fine motor skills needed for writing. This is a multi-sensory experience with lots of opportunity for language and creative development.

# Making a swing

## What you need:

- Some rope, at least 5 mm thick
- A heavy object, such as a small rock
- A tree branch, strong enough to hold your weight
- A tyre, plank of wood or a smooth, reasonably fat stick

## What to do:

1. Choose a place where you cannot swing into anything, for example the tree itself.

2. Once you have found a suitable tree, get your rope and your heavy object. Tie the end of the rope to the object and throw it up over your chosen branch.

3. Take the other end of the rope and tie a strong loop.

4. Untie the object from the rope and feed the end of it through the loop and pull. The end with the loop should get pulled up to the branch and form a strong fastening.

5. Tie your stick, plank or tyre to the end of the rope securely.

6. Check the rope is securely fastened to the branch by pulling down hard on the rope before using your swing.

### Top tip ⭐

You could also double up the rope instead of tying a loop, but you end up with two ends of rope.

### Taking it forward

- By taking away the 'seat' and providing just a knot at the end of the rope, children will have to work hard to stay on, using their core muscles and upper body strength.

### What's in it for the children?

Swinging is fun and exciting. The feeling of the wind rushing in your face and the feeling of being weightless is a thrill for any child. Swinging, spinning and other movement through space helps children's brain development and their ability to concentrate by stimulating their vestibular system.

### Health & Safety

Make sure that the branch that you are using is not dead or dying and that the rope is tied securely. Supervise this activity at all times.

# Puddle Pictures

## What you need:

- Puddles
- Wellies
- Powder paint
- Glitter, flower petals,
- Chalk
- Pestle and mortar

## Top tip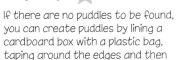

If there are no puddles to be found, you can create puddles by lining a cardboard box with a plastic bag, taping around the edges and then filling it with water.

## What to do:

1. Go outside on a rainy day and look for big puddles.

2. Sprinkle some powder paint on the surface and stir with a stick to create a different effect.

3. Add petals, glitter and leaves to complete your puddle picture.

4. Explore objects that will float on the puddles: leaves, small sticks, feathers etc.

5. Use chalks to colour the puddles. Let the children crush the chalk under foot or use a pestle and mortar to grind them up and then add to their puddles.

### Taking it forward

- When the children have finished their puddle pictures they can use a broom to sweep their pictures away. Art can be both beautiful and temporary!

### What's in it for the children?

This activity allows children to experiment with colour and design on an ever-changing canvas.

## Health & Safety

Always supervise children around water.

# Mud paint

## What you need:

- Mud or container of top soil
- Buckets
- Spoons
- Muffin tins or other containers
- Water
- Powder paint or food colouring in containers with small scoops
- Paintbrushes (try using the Nature's paintbrushes on page 8)
- Large sheets or rolls of paper

## What to do:

1. Ask the children to collect mud in their buckets if you have a ready supply in your setting or offer a large container of top soil.

2. Let the children fill each hole of the muffin tin and experiment with adding water to make different 'recipes'. What happens if you add a little mud and lots of water?

3. The mud can be used with or without adding colour, but this is a great opportunity for exploring colour mixing.

4. Offer the children large sheets or rolls of paper on the ground to paint on.

Top tip ⭐

Offer the children the opportunity to paint on a vertical surface to enable optimum movement of the shoulder, elbow and to develop the wrist pivot.

Encourage the children to write down their own recipes including measures – 2 spoonfuls of mud, 1 spoonful of water, 3 scoops of red powder paint etc.

### Vhat's in it for the children?

his activity introduces the children to he mathematical concept of measuring nd allows exploration of the early cience notion of cause and effect by reating their own paint mixtures. By etting up this activity outdoors the hildren can paint on a much larger cale than would be possible in a assroom.

# Grass caterpillars

## What you need:

- Recycled nylon stockings or tights
- Soil
- Grass seeds
- Rubber bands
- Water
- Scissors

**Top tip** ⭐

Keep the soil moist but not wet whilst the seeds are growing.

## What to do:

1. Cut the stockings to a length of about 30 cm.
2. Mix one cup of soil to one cup of grass seed.
3. Ask the children to fill the stockings with the soil and grass seed mix.
4. Use the rubber bands to seal the end.
5. Get the children to soak the 'caterpillars' in water.
6. Ask the children to add any features – drawn on or stuck on googly eyes, antennae etc.
7. In less than three days you will see the seeds start to germinate. After five to six days you should have pretty hairy caterpillars!
8. Encourage the children to use scissors to give their caterpillars a trim.

### Taking it forward

- Try herb instead of grass seeds, which the children will later be able to harvest to use in salads and sandwiches.

### What's in it for the children?

This activity is a great way for children to learn about growing. They can talk about the roots, shoots and leaves. They can make observations of their plant and talk about change over time.

# Stick wands

## What you need:

- Sticks
- Objects collected from a walk
- Pipe cleaners

## What to do:

1. Go for a walk in the woods and ask each child to choose a stick for themselves.

2. Search around on the ground for interesting things to attach to the wand. There are many different shapes and textures to choose from.

3. Give each child a pipe cleaner to wrap around the natural objects they have found and attach them to the top of the stick.

4. What spells can the children create?

### What's in it for the children?

This activity allows children to introduce a storyline or narrative into their play. They can listen to others and express their own ideas during their imaginative play.

### Taking it forward

- Get the children to use their magic wands to create their own magic potions. Offer them a range of different ingredients to add. Try including lemon juice and bicarbonate of soda for a bubbling reaction!

## Top tip ⭐

Look out for seeds fallen from trees that make a sound when you shake them!

# Natural object animals

## What you need:

- Selection of different sized pine cones
- Acorns, leaves, twigs, feathers
- Googly eyes
- String or pipe cleaners

### Top tip ⭐

Explore the theme with the children by reading some stories about woodland animals to give them some ideas about the range and types of animals in this environment.

## What to do:

1. Go outside and gather some natural treasures.

2. Allow the children plenty of time to explore the resources.

3. What animals can they make? What features do they have? Invite the children to make a range of different sized animals and encourage them to consider what features to add to differentiate each animal.

### Taking it forward

- Get the children to make a whole family of animals and use them to enhance small world play in your setting.

### What's in it for the children?

Creative activities can help children to create critical thinking skills. Using natural resources such as these provides opportunities for children to use all their senses while developing an understanding of growth, decay and change.

# Natural mandalas

- A selection of objects to make a pattern such as shells, leaves, seeds, conkers, sticks, pebbles, flower heads etc.

### Mandala

'Mandala' (Sanskrit for 'circle') is a spiritual and ritual symbol in Hinduism and Buddhism, representing the Universe. The basic form of most mandalas is a circle containing a square with four gates, which in turn contain a circular centre point.

## What to do:

1. Show the children some images of mandalas (there are lots of different ones online) and explain what they represent.

2. Choose a flat surface to arrange your mandalas – floor, table top, etc.

3. Ask the children to select an interesting object to be their centre piece.

4. Encourage the children to arrange the other objects around the centre piece to make their pattern.

### Taking it forward

- Give the children a camera and ask them to photograph their mandala. You could collate them to make a book and add some written descriptions.

### What's in it for the children?

Handling small objects helps children to develop hand-eye coordination. Exploring art in this way enables children to develop an understanding of colour, size, shape and texture.

### Top tip

Creating the mandalas in trays will enable the children to leave the activity to revisit and improve later.

# Leaf bugs

## What you need:

- Colourful leaves of different shapes and sizes, sticks, twigs, seeds, fir cones, acorns, feathers etc.
- PVA glue
- Card squares

## Top tip ⭐

Only collect things that have fallen from the trees and are on the ground. Do not break branches or pick wild flowers.

**Health & Safety**

Never visit woods on a really windy day.

## What to do:

1. Discuss which different types of insects the children know. Look at how many legs, wings and body parts they have.
2. Go out for a walk to gather a collection of leaves and other natural resources to create pictures.
3. Allow the children to explore the resources and let their imaginations go wild creating their own leaf creatures.
4. Make a class display.

### Taking it forward

- Try offering similar resources on the play dough table to see what 3D creatures the children can create.
- Can the children make up a name for their leaf bug?

### What's in it for the children?

This would be an ideal activity to go along with any minibeast interest. It will encourage discussion around the features and body parts of insects.

# Mud Pizzas

## What you need:

- A supply of mud or top soil
- **Empty pizza boxes** (ask your local pizza delivery restaurant)
- **Herbs, leaves, bark, orange peel, sawdust and flower petals etc. for toppings**
- Access to water
- **Utensils for stirring, slicing, mashing**
- **Whiteboards and dry wipe pens**
- Play telephone for taking orders

## What to do:

1. Allow the children to mix the soil with water, exploring different textures.
2. Let them have fun moulding the mud into balls and then flattening them into pizza shapes in the boxes.
3. Give them the resources to create their own concoctions.

### Top tip

Play alongside the children, providing them with new vocabulary such as sprinkle, grind, concoctions, mixture etc.

### Taking it forward

- Add a pestle and mortar to grind up leaves, seeds and flowers. Offer the children the whiteboards and pens to encourage them to write down recipes, menus and orders.

### What's in it for the children?

Playing with mud offers a great sensory experience. It provides opportunities for experimenting and discovery whilst inspiring creativity and developing gross and fine motor skills through stirring, moulding and manipulating the mud.

### ✚ Health & Safety

Ensure that the soil is not contaminated with any animal faeces and that the children wash their hands thoroughly after playing with mud.

# Den building

## What you need:

- Tarpaulin or fabric
- Clamps or pegs
- String or masking tape
- Bamboo canes or branches

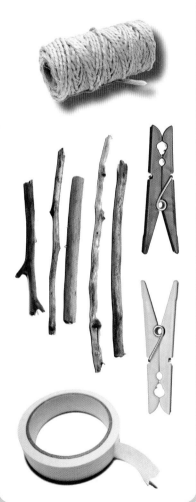

## What to do:

1. Ask the children where they want to build their den.
2. Help them gather together the materials they need.
3. Support them to construct their dens, allowing them to make all the decisions on its design.
4. Leave the den set up for a couple of days so that the children can revisit and extend their play.

## Top tip ⭐

Add cushions and blankets to make the den cosy.

- After making a couple of dens with the children, have all of the resources available so that they can construct dens independently.

## What's in it for the children?

Dens can offer a safe and cosy space for imaginative play and provide some fantastic opportunities for communication and language development. Children will need to listen to each other's ideas and work together collaboratively to complete their den.

# Bird feeder

## What to do:

1. Help the children to attach some string to the pine cones.
2. Gently heat the suet in the microwave until melted (adult only).
3. Ask the children to mix equal amounts of melted suet (not too hot) with oats, then spread the mixture onto the pine cone with spoons or fingers.
4. Pour the bird seed into the tray and get the children to roll the pine cones in the bird seed to coat.
5. Hang the feeders from a tree branch.

### Taking it forward

- Allow the children to take their bird feeder home to hang. Encourage them to keep a record of the different types of birds that visit their feeder.

- Provide materials to help the children learn more about birds: bird spotting books, binoculars, abandoned bird's nests, feathers etc.

### What's in it for the children?

Taking responsibility for feeding birds is a social skill, especially when shared with classmates. Watching birds encourages observation skills, can help to instil the value and significance of the natural world and exposes children to the importance of non-fiction resources.

## Top tip ⭐

Try to hang the feeders away from the trunk of trees so it's more difficult for squirrels to get at them.

# Nature wristbands

## What you need:

- Gaffer tape
- Selection of natural items

## Top tip ⭐

Leave the gaffer tape loose enough to be able to slide it off the children's wrists or have room to cut it off.

## What to do:

1. Wrap a strip of gaffer tape around the children's wrists, sticky side out.

2. Go for a walk and see what natural treasures the children can find to stick on to their wristband.

3. Smaller things work best, but the gaffer tape should be sticky enough to hold slightly heavier things like small stones or pieces of bark.

### Taking it forward

- You could collect objects on a theme, for example a certain colour or give the children a list of things to find.

### What's in it for the children?

The expectation in this activity is that the children look carefully in their environment and notice small details that may otherwise be missed. This activity helps children to develop their hand-eye coordination and encourages them to think about the size and weight of objects to determine whether or not they would be suitable for their wristband.

# Stick silhouette

## What you need:

- Sticks of different lengths
- A clear space to lie down

### Top tip ⭐

To get the idea of a silhouette, the children could draw around each other on paper before attempting this activity.

## What to do:

1. Have the children working in pairs. The first child finds somewhere to lie down.

2. Their partner arranges sticks around them, following the shape of their body. Remind them to find the correct length of stick as they place them around their friend's body, end to end.

3. Once finished, partner one carefully stands up without disturbing the sticks, to reveal their body silhouette on the ground.

4. They swap roles.

### Taking it forward

- Can they use leaves, acorns, conkers, flowers etc. to create the facial features? What could they use for the hair?

### What's in it for the children?

This activity gives children first-hand experience of length by looking at perimeter. How many sticks have they used? Can they estimate how many sticks they would need to complete their teacher's silhouette? Are all sticks the same length?

# Mud creatures

## What you need:

- Wet mud
- Natural objects for features

## Top tip

Print off some images of different creatures to inspire the children and watch as they create their own.

## Health & Safety

Make sure there is no rubbish or animal mess.

## What to do:

1. Encourage the children to mould the sticky mud to make the body shape of their creature.

2. Then use the natural objects to add features such as legs, wings, teeth, tentacles, eyes, claws etc.

3. Talk about different features and encourage the children to make accurate representations.

### Taking it forward

- Replace the mud with clay which has more resistance and its own properties. The children will be able to dry and keep the models they have made.

### What's in it for the children?

Moulding mud in your hands is calming and therapeutic. Rolling, squeezing and forming the mud helps to develop children's fine motor skills.

# Creating a fairy glen

## What you need:

- Some twigs, leaves and any other natural treasures
- A generous amount of glitter
- Miniature chalk boards and chalk

## What to do:

1. Let the children find a location for their fairy house.

2. Ask the children to collect the resources they need: leaves, twigs, pebbles, pine cones, feathers, moss and shells etc.

3. Allow them to construct their fairy homes, asking them about their design and the reasons for the resources they have selected.

4. Ask them to think about the entrance to their home. Does it need a pathway or a special magical gate? Who will live in their home? A family of pixies, a lone fairy?

5. When they have completed their construction, allow them to sprinkle the area with glittery fairy dust to help the fairies to find their way there!

**Top tip** ⭐

Start the activity off with a tiny letter from a fairy or pixie asking for the children's help to build some new homes.

**Taking it forward**

- The children could design and make some furniture and clothes for the fairies using natural objects.

- Give them the chalk boards and ask them to name their fairy homes, Pixie Palace, Elfful Tower etc.

**What's in it for the children?**

Construction supports and strengthens problem solving and concentration skills. Children grow in confidence when they experience a sense of purpose and achievement. Constructing in this miniature way supports dexterity and fine motor development.

# Sky gazing

## What you need:

- A dry day
- A rug or blanket to lie on

## What to do:

1. Take the children outside and watch the clouds drifting across the sky.

2. Notice that no two clouds are the same and that they are constantly changing.

3. Talk about the shapes that they can see. Remember that there are no right or wrong answers.

4. Ask the children if they can guess which way the wind is blowing by watching how the clouds are moving.

5. How many different types of cloud can you find out about together? Cumulus clouds look heaped and fluffy. Cirrus clouds are high and wispy.

### Taking it forward

- Ask the children to take turns to describe a shape that they can see. Can the other children point to that cloud shape?

- Set the children the task of looking at the night sky with their families.

### What's in it for the children?

Cloud gazing is both fun and relaxing and it also provides a stimulus for imagination and communication.

# Tree hugging

## What you need:

- Blindfolds
- A wooded area

## What to do:

1. Put children into pairs, with one child being blindfolded and the other the leader.

2. Explain to the children that they will need to listen carefully to their partner, as they are lead from the starting point to a nearby tree.

3. Once the pair have reached a tree, the blindfolded partner needs to place their hands on the tree to feel its texture and any patterns etc.

4. They can stretch up to see if they can reach any branches and hug the tree to get an idea of its circumference.

5. The leader will take them back to the starting point and the child will remove their blindfold

6. Can the child identify which tree they were hugging? How do they know?

7. The leader will say if they are correct. They can then swap roles.

### Taking it forward

- Explore other senses through tasting, smelling and listening games.

### What's in it for the children?

is good to offer children the opportunity to actively explore their world using their senses. This activity develops good relationships as children learn to trust each other. Children will be using two-channelled attention as they have to listen to complete the task.

### Health & Safety

Choose an area with no exposed roots or low overhanging branches.

# Worm charming

## What you need:

- A garden fork
- Musical instruments
- Balls
- Watering can with rose attachment
- Washing-up liquid
- Paper and clipboards to record findings
- A container with damp soil to keep collected worms in the dark

## Top tip

You are more likely to find worms during the warmer months, between March and October.

## Taking it forward

- Encourage the children to find a method of presenting their results so that others can understand them: will they choose a drawing, a chart, a table or a graph? Did the vibrations work better than methods using water?

- To take the investigation further and keep some worms in your classroom, you can buy worm habitats over the internet. (www.insectlore.co.uk)

## What's in it for the children?

This helps the children to identify features of a particular habitat and allows them the opportunity to observe worms closely, explaining what they see. This also introduces children to data handling when they record how many worms they find.

## What to do:

1. Tell the children they are going to investigate worms, and that they will begin by trying different techniques to charm the worms! Where do the children predict they will find the most worms and why do they think this? What is it about that particular habitat that the worms might like? Discuss how worms should be handled gently and returned to their habitat afterwards.

2. Worms are sensitive to sound vibrations and will come to the surface if they are subjected to the right kind of noise. Try any of the following methods:

   - stamping feet and drumming hands on the ground (known as the Seagull Dance!)
   - playing musical instruments
   - bouncing balls on the ground
   - sticking a garden fork into the ground and hitting the handle with a stick
   - using a watering can to sprinkle water mixed with a little washing-up liquid into the ground (rinse the worms in clean water when they come to the surface).

3. Record how many worms appear after trying each technique.

4. Release the worms somewhere dark and damp.

# Imaginary animal walk

## What you need:

- Walk in local woodlands
- Safety mirror for each child

## What to do:

1. Find a local wood to explore or an area within a park with lots of trees.

2. Give each child a mirror to hold flat in the palm of their hand.

3. Encourage the children to look in the mirror to see the reflection of the canopy above. Can they describe what they see?

4. Ask them to imagine they are a woodland animal. How would they move?

5. As they walk along, can they use the mirror to find a place to shelter, build a nest or a den? Can they find something to eat?

6. Place all the mirrors together on the ground to capture the woodland scene.

### Taking it forward

Back at your setting find some music and ask the children to represent their ideas through dance and music, thinking about how their animal would move and react to each other.

### What's in it for the children?

This encourages children to look up and explore the world from a different perspective. It opens discussion about reflections, mirror image and symmetry.

### Health & Safety

Risk assess the woodland area to ensure there are no trip hazards. Work with small groups of children.

# Bug hunt

## What you need:

- Non-fiction books on minibeasts
- A print out of common insects
- Small pots
- Magnifying glasses
- Clipboard
- Paper and pens
- Camera

## What to do:

1. Offer the children the non-fiction books on minibeasts and look at the similarities and differences of a selection of minibeasts. Can they name any minibeasts or talk about their features?

2. Explain to the children the need to be gentle.

3. Go outside to search for minibeasts. Show the children how to carefully lift logs, look inside bark crevices in trees and under stones and leaves to see what creatures they can find.

4. Can the children identify and draw the minibeasts they have spotted?

5. Help the children to describe their features. e.g. how many legs does it have? How does it move? Can it fly?

6. Encourage them to record their findings using the camera.

### Taking it forward

- Make a class book to include their pictures and photos of minibeasts. Can the children label the creature's body parts and talk about their habitats?

### What's in it for the children?

This activity offers children the opportunity to explore and identify different minibeasts, classifying the minibeasts that have wings, legs, markings etc. By taking care to return them to their natural habitat, the children gain some understanding of their own influence on living things and the environment.

### Top tip ⭐

Ensure all creatures are handled sensitively and released safely at the end of the activity.

# Herby soup

## What you need:

- Large container of water
- Bunches of herbs, mint, basil, rosemary, chives, oregano, etc.
- Bowls
- Scissors
- Pestle and mortar
- Spoons

**Top tip** ⭐

Add rotary and balloon whisks to increase gross motor development.

## What to do:

1. Discuss with the children their understanding of herbs and allow them to explore the different fragrances by crushing them between fingers.

2. Offer the children scissors to snip the herbs into their bowls and the pestle and mortar for grinding.

3. They can add water with scoops or ladles.

### Taking it forward

- Grow your own herb garden for a ready supply of herbs for the children to access.

- Use mint with garlic, cucumber and yoghurt to make tzatziki dip with the children.

### What's in it for the children?

Water play is fundamental to children's early development of mathematics and science concepts. It provides opportunities for children to strengthen their physical skills, develop their social and emotional skills and enrich their language development.

# Stick wind chimes

## What you need:

- A selection of sticks
- Some screw eyes
- Garden string
- A colander

## Top tip ⭐

Sticks of different lengths and widths will create a variety of sound.

## What to do:

1. Help the children to screw the metal eyes into the centre of the stick at one end, you may need to start them off, then they should be able to screw them in to the stick as far as they will go.

2. Show the children where to thread the string through the colander and help them to tie a knot.

3. Let the children thread the other end through the eye on the stick and, again help them to tie a knot. (They could use tape to secure the string independently.)

4. Keep going until all the sticks are hanging from the colander and then decide with the children where to hang the finished 'wind chime'.

### Taking it forward

- Design a really large frame, using lengths of bamboo, so that the children can create music by running between and through the sticks.

### What's in it for the children?

Every child can enjoy music, regardless of age or background. Wind chimes are a calming addition to any setting and the sounds they produce also encourage the children to think and talk about the wind and its effects.

# Leave a trail

## What you need:

- A walk in the local woods
- Some images of trail signs (try scouting websites)
- Two groups of children, with an adult supporting each group
- Some natural resources to practise agreed signs with

## What to do:

1. Before setting off, look through the images and natural resources and decide together what each symbol will mean.

2. Once you arrive in your wooded area, one group will go off and set the trail, while the other group can gather resources for their trail.

3. After an agreed amount of time, the second group will set off, following the trail to find their friends.

4. Questions to ask along the trail: Which way do we need to go now? What could this mean? What other clues can we use? (footprints, noise, natural obstacles etc.).

## Top tip

Don't make the trails too long in order to keep the children interested.

### Taking it forward

- Give the children a checklist of things to find along the trail.

### What's in it for the children?

Trails provide important opportunities for children to access, experience and learn about nature. During this activity we can teach directional words and phrases such as above and below, turn left, turn right and go straight ahead to help the children with the concept of location.

# Building dams

## What you need:

- Shallow trays
- Sand
- Small rocks
- Sticks
- Bucket of water

## Top tip ⭐

Show the children some images of man-made and beaver-made dams to fuel their imagination and help with their understanding.

## What to do:

1. Explain to the children that a dam is a structure that stops water flowing. Set them a challenge to build their own dam.

2. Fill the trays with sand.

3. Get the children to dig a path for the river with their hands or tools.

4. Let them decide where they want to position their dam. Then use the sticks and rocks to construct their dam.

5. Once they are satisfied their dam's ready, test its effectiveness by tilting the tray and pouring water down the river path.

6. Did the dam work? Do they need to make some adjustments to their dam?

7. Remember that the more water poured on, the greater the pressure, so the bottom of the dam needs to be stronger than the top. Is it more effective if the dam is triangular in shape?

**Taking it forward**

- Build dams on a larger scale in the sand tray or better still in a sand pit, working together to construct a barrier.

**What's in it for the children?**

This activity offers an opportunity to talk about engineering. Dams are used for irrigation, storing drinking water, making electricity and they also control flooding. Throughout this task children will be constructing with a purpose in mind, selecting appropriate resources and adapting their designs.

# Creating small world environments

## What you need:

- Tyres
- Planters
- Raised flower beds
- Soil
- Natural materials for landscaping such as rocks, bark, gravel, logs
- Small hardy plants such as rockery plants, succulents, herbs etc.
- Other naturals resources such as conkers, sticks, pebbles, acorn cups, fir cones etc.

## What to do:

1. Chose where you want to position your small world environment. You may want to put two or three (tyres for example) together and create different worlds in each.

2. Create the scene by filling the container with soil and adding objects of differing heights and textures to add interest.

3. Add the plants to soften the landscape and keep it natural.

4. Enhance with small baskets of moss, glass nuggets, acorn cups, sticks, pebbles and small world figures for the children to create and design their own magical worlds.

### Taking it forward

- To extend play further, add battery operated tea lights and safely position a large mirror behind.

### What's in it for the children?

Small world play increases creativity and imagination. Children begin to work out their own problems and issues through their characters. Small world offers fantastic opportunities for language development and provides the children with foundations for storytelling.

### Top tip ⭐

Include small world environments that are perfect for one child to explore as well as some larger spaces where children can play collaboratively.

# Natural bubble wands

## What you need:

- Some vines or freshly cut branches
- Raffia or string
- Washing-up liquid
- Glycerine
- Water
- Large shallow container

## Top tip

When you dip the wand into the liquid, do not agitate the mixture too much.

## What to do:

**1.** Bend the end of a thin stick or branch over to make a loop.

**2.** Tie it tightly with the string, making different sized loops to create different sized bubbles.

**3.** In the tray, add a couple of centimetres of water, a squirt of washing-up liquid and half the bottle of glycerine. The more glycerine and washing-up liquid you add, the more effective the bubbles.

**4.** Dip the wands into the mixture and slowly lift out, then gently blow or wave to form bubbles.

**5.** Ask the children questions such as: 'If we use a square wand, will we get square bubbles?', 'What colours can you see?', 'Where did the colours come from?'

**6.** Use vocabulary such as float, burst, surface tension, weight, light etc. when playing alongside the children.

### Taking it forward

- Try making a huge loop to see if you can form an enormous bubble.

- Experiment with different shaped loops; notice that the bubbles are always round.

### What's in it for the children?

Oral motor skills are being developed when blowing bubbles. Blowing bubbles also enables children to practise hand-eye coordination and tracking the bubbles will promote concentration and attention.

# Herb banks

## What you need:

- Large buckets with drainage holes
- Some established herbs
- Herb seeds
- Potting compost
- Trowels
- Small watering cans

## Taking it forward

- Once the herb banks are established, tie some scissors to the handles and place them near your mud kitchen or apothecary area for the children to access independently.

## What to do:

1. Ask the children to fill the buckets with compost within 5 cm of the top.
2. Get the children to dig small holes to plant the established herbs.
3. They can use their fingers to poke small hole for the seeds.
4. Show the children how to gently cover over the seeds with compost.
5. Let the children give the buckets a good soak with the watering cans.
6. Place them in a warm, sunny position.
7. Give the children the responsibility of watering the herbs when necessary.

### What's in it for the children?

Children will have hands-on experience of growing plants. It offers the opportunity to discuss roots, stems and leaves, as well as what plants need to grow. By allowing the children to harvest their own herbs you are promoting independence in your setting and giving them the responsibility of caring for their learning environment.

# Story stones

## What you need:

- Stones
- Images of characters from classic stories for example: *The Gruffalo*, *The Three Little Pigs* etc.
- PVA glue
- Clear varnish

## Top tip ⭐

Make sure the children have had some exposure to the stories and characters.

## What to do:

1. Choose your stones to fit the images.
2. Cut around the pictures and glue onto the stones with the PVA.
3. Give each stone a coat of clear varnish to protect it.
4. Make them available to the children alongside a copy of the story.

### Taking it forward

- Leave some stones and pens out for children to create their own characters.
- Make some stones with images of the children in your setting, so they can include themselves and their friends in their stories.

### What's in it for the children?

Retelling a story encourages children to picture the storyline and characters in their heads. Storytelling promotes expressive language development and gives the children the opportunity to try out new vocabulary, refining their understanding.

# Dream catcher

## What you need:

- Long bendy sticks that will not break when bent into a circle
- String or wool
- Feathers, ribbons, shells, pine cones etc.

## Top tip

Be aware that this may open further discussion. Be sensitive to what the children are saying.

## What to do:

1. Open the discussion by sharing a book about fears – try *Little Mouse's Big Book of Fears* by Emily Gravett.

2. In small groups, allow the children to share any fears they might have.

3. Invite the children to come and make their very own dream catcher to take home to catch bad dreams.

4. Gently bend the stick to create a circle and tie together in several positions around the circle to ensure they don't come apart.

5. Ask the children to wind the string around the frame.

6. The children can select items to tie onto their dream catcher.

### Taking it forward

Provide wooden dolly pegs for the children to make sets of worry dolls to use in the classroom. Children can come and whisper any fears to them.

### What's in it for the children?

By talking about their fears, children will begin to understand how to manage their feelings in a safe and supported environment. When children feel they have been heard and acknowledged they may find the confidence to share more with you.

# Bow and arrows

## What you need:

- Sturdy but flexible branches or sticks, approximately 75 cm in length
- Hot glue gun (adult supervision required)
- Thick cord elastic, twine or heavy-duty string
- Duct tape
- Straight sticks for the arrows
- Cotton wool or some sort of padding for the tip (so the ends do not have a sharp point)
- Wooden lolly sticks

## What to do:

1. To construct the bow, tie one end of elastic to the end of the stick about 2 cm down from the end.
2. Two people will be needed, one to hold the tied end of the stick and the other to pull the untied end into a curved bow shape.
3. Tie the other end of the elastic to the other end of the bow. Make sure the elastic is tied tight enough to create the bow shape.
4. Experiment with the pull of the bow. If it is too loose, wrap the elastic around a couple of times, until you get the desired tension.
5. Secure the tied ends with duct tape.
6. In the middle of the bow, wrap a length of duct tape to create a shelf for the arrow.
7. The arrow needs to be at least twice the length of the distance between the string and the centre of the bow's bend.
8. Get the children to place a ball of cotton wool on the end of the stick, wrap it in fabric and secure the ends of the fabric to the stick using duct tape.
9. Cut a lolly stick in half and glue one side on either side of the arrow body with about 2 cm sticking past the back end of the stick to create a 'notch'.
10. Secure the lolly sticks with duct tape.
11. Set up targets for the children and set them challenges.

➕ **Health & Safety**

Set out firm ground rules about bow and arrow use. Mark out an area where the children can practise their archery skills safely, where other children will not be in the firing line.

- Create an archery tournament for the children to compete in.

- Can they work in teams? Can the children decide how points will be scored?

Vhat's in it for the children?

archery is physically demanding, developing the children's pper body strength. It also demands concentration, so nproves attention skills.

# Willow Crowns

## What you need:

- Lengths of freshly cut willow, long enough to wrap around a child's head twice.
- Tape or string
- Flower heads
- Ivy
- Leaves
- Ribbons or streamers
- Long grasses
- Feathers

## What to do:

1. Wrap the willow around the child's head once and as it overlaps weave the rest of the willow over and under until it is all woven in. Secure the end with tape or string.

2. Allow the children to select their chosen resources to weave into their crown.

### Taking it forward

- Can the children create a story and perform an open-air show in their crowns?

### What's in it for the children?

Children can develop their own ideas through selecting the materials they want to incorporate into their crown. Encourage them to talk about their design and reasons for choice.

# Matching nature's colours

## What you need:

- A selection of colour sample cards from DIY shops
- Hole punch
- Camera

## Top tip ⭐

Hole-punch the colour cards and tie a selection together to make it easier for the children to carry.

## What to do:

1. Hand out a selection of the colour samples to the children. Talk about the range of colours and shades of similar colours.

2. Take the children to an outdoor area.

3. As you are walking along encourage the children to look out for things to match with the colours on the cards.

4. Give the children a camera to record their findings.

## Taking it forward

Can the children create their own colours? Mark out 100 squares on a sheet of paper and challenge the children to create 100 different colours and shades by mixing paint in palettes.

## What's in it for the children?

This is not just an activity for colour, but an exploration on colour and shade. It allows children to experiment with not only primary and secondary colours, but also tertiary and quadrary colours. Language and literacy can be explored with books such as *Mouse Paint* by Ellen Stoll Walsh and *White Rabbit's Colour Book* by Ann Baker.

fantastic ideas for exploring nature

# Seasonal jars

## What you need:

- Empty jars
- Water
- Oil
- Glitter
- Food colouring
- Natural treasures such as conkers, fir cones, twigs and leaves collected from outside

## Top tip ⭐

Mark '¾' and 'full' on the side of the jars to help the children to complete this independently.

### Taking it forward

- Create jars for each season, looking at the natural resources you will find at various times throughout the year. Ask the children to choose their colours to represent each season.

### What's in it for the children?

This introduces children to the basic scientific concept of floating by engaging their interest. It encourages children to talk about why some things occur and change.

### ✚ Health & Safety

You may choose to use plastic jars rather than glass.

## What to do:

1. Ask the children to fill the jars three quarters full with water, then top it up with oil.

2. Let the children add glitter and observe what happens.

3. Offer them the food colouring to add. How does it react with the oil? Does it mix with the oil or water?

4. The children can then add their treasures to the jars.

5. Ask the children to predict what will happen.

6. Questions to ask: Will the oil and water mix? Does the glitter float or sink? Will the conkers, fir cones, twigs and leaves float or sink?

7. Screw on the lids, give the mixture a shake and watch what happens.